Travel Guide To

Okavango Delta

Tony D. Lawson

Explore The Tranquil Waterways of The Okavango Delta With Lions, Leopards, Rhinos and Many Others On Sight.

Table Of Contents

Chapter 1

Introduction

1.1 Welcome to the Okavango Delta

- A Natural Wonder: The Okavango Delta
- Presenting the Okavango Delta as one of nature's most extraordinary and magnificent beauties.
- Drawing attention to the fact that it is a UNESCO World Heritage Site.
- A Haven for Lovers of the Natural World
- describing the fauna, biodiversity, and beautiful landscapes of the Delta.
- Inviting readers to experience the unique peace and beauty of the Delta.
10 Reasons to Visit the Okavango Delta
- Highlighting the best attractions, including cultural experiences and wildlife excursions.

- Emphasizing the destination's once-in-a-lifetime status.

1.2 This Travel Guide's Overview

- Your Reliable Friend
- Outlining the objective of this book as a thorough travel resource.
- Assuring readers that it's created to improve their experience of the Okavango Delta.
- What You'll Discover
- Giving a summary of the guide's contents and structure.
- Hinting to the content readers might anticipate, such as travel advice and cultural insights.
- Using the Guide.
- Providing tips on how to use the handbook to its fullest, including how to use the table of contents.

- Encouraging readers to go further into the portions that interest them.

1.3 Travel Planning

- The Beginning of the Journey
- Emphasizing the need for thorough travel preparation.
- Motivating readers to begin their trip by comprehending what is in store for them.
- When to Visit.
- A discussion on the value of visiting the Okavango Delta at the appropriate time.
- Disseminating knowledge on seasonal differences and how they affect the experience.

Establishing Expectations
- Setting realistic expectations for visitors by emphasizing the Delta's wild and secluded setting.

- Mentioning the lack of network connection and urban amenities.
- Sustainable Development and Safe Travel
- Stressing the guide's dedication to safe travel.
- Inspiring readers to reduce their environmental footprint and support their local communities.
- Planning Requirements
- Outlining the fundamentals of vacation preparation, from financial factors to travel documents.
- Emphasizing the value of doing your research on lodgings and activities.

What Comes Next
- Setting the tone for the remainder of the guide by emphasizing the parts that follow.
- Hinting to the information and adventure that will be revealed in the next chapters.

This thorough introduction is intended to acquaint readers with the Okavango Delta, establish the tone for the trip manual, and get them ready for the organizing process.

Chapter 2

Having knowledge of the Okavango Delta

2.1 Location and Geography

The Okavango Delta is where?

- Giving readers a description of the Okavango Delta's location inside Botswana, in Africa.

- Providing information about its closeness to other renowned areas or attractions.

- An Unparalleled Delta

- Explaining the distinctive creation of the Delta, which is defined by an inland delta system.

- Outlining its unique characteristics and how the Okavango River supplies it.

- The Varying Terrain
- Outlining the many ecosystems present in the Delta, such as islands, floodplains, and woods.
- Showcasing the impact these settings have on animals and the experience of visitors.

2.2 Ecosystem and Biodiversity

- A Wilderness World
- Outlining the Okavango Delta's remarkable biodiversity, which includes both well-known and obscure species.
- Examining the value of the Delta as a haven for threatened and endangered species.

- The Function of the Ecosystem
- Outlining the biological processes that support the rich animals of the Delta.

- Talking about the yearly flood cycle and how it affects the ecology.
- Paradise for Birdwatchers
- Highlighting the Delta's importance as a hub for bird watching.
- Showcasing some of the most prized bird species that live in the Delta.

2.3 Cultural Significance

- The Native Americans
- Examining the San people and the long history of human occupancy in the Delta.
- Examining their ties to the environment and traditional way of life.

- Intercultural Exchanges
- Talking about ways that tourists may interact with local people and discover their way of life.

- Providing details on cultural encounters and trips.

- Maintaining Customs
- Stressing the significance of sustainable tourism methods and cultural preservation.
- Encouraging visitors to support and appreciate the local way of life.

- Botswana's Use of the Delta
- Emphasizing the Okavango Delta's importance to Botswana in terms of both culture and economy.
- Talking about conservation initiatives and the Delta's significance to national identity.

This section attempts to provide readers with a thorough grasp of the geographical characteristics, the rich environment, and the cultural significance of the Okavango Delta. It lays the groundwork for a more engaging and knowledgeable travel experience.

Chapter 3

How to Get There

3.1 Transportation and Entry Points

How to get to the Okavango Delta

- An introduction to the several entrances and gates to the Delta, such as Kasane, Maun, and others.

- Details on how to get from well-known international airports to these entrance locations on connecting flights.

- Selecting a Transportation Method

- Looking at possible modes of transportation, including small aircraft, road transfers, and boat transfers.

- Talking about the experiences and conveniences related to each method.

- Getting Around the Delta

- Knowing how to use several modes of transportation to go about the Delta, such as game drives and mokoros (dugout canoes).

- Emphasizing the experience of navigating across narrow canals on traditional mokoros.

3.2 Entry Requirements and Visas

- Visa and Passport Requirements

- Giving passengers comprehensive information on passport expiration dates and visa requirements.

- Providing assistance in obtaining visas either in advance of travel or on arrival in Botswana.

- Exemptions & Waivers for Visas
- Talking about nations that could have eased entrance criteria or visa waivers.
- A recommendation to readers to check the most recent visa requirements before their journey.

- Safety measures and vaccinations
- Educating visitors on the mandatory health measures, immunizations, and entry-level medical documentation.
- Addressing any health issues connected to visiting the Delta.

3.3 Visit at the Best Time

- Considerations for the Season
- A description of the Okavango Delta's several seasons, including the dry season, rainy season, and shoulder seasons.

- Talking about the impact these seasons have on animal observations and activity.

- Timing for Wildlife Viewing
- Offering suggestions for the best times to go on game drives and watch wildlife while taking into account animal behavior patterns.
- Stressing how exciting it is to see the yearly flood and its effects on the Delta's scenery.

- Preferable Climate
- Providing details on seasonal weather trends to assist tourists in selecting proper clothing.
- Addressing probable precipitation and temperature changes.

- Festivals and Special Events

- Showcasing any unusual animal or cultural occurrences that take place at certain periods of the year.

- Encouraging visitors to time their trip to coincide with these occasions for a more enriching experience.

This section provides useful information to aid visitors in planning their trip to the Okavango Delta, including advice on picking the best entrance ports and modes of transportation, comprehending visa requirements, and deciding when to go depending on their interests and preferences.

Chapter 4

Accommodation

4.1 Camps and Lodges

- Expensive Safari Lodges
- A description of the upscale safari lodges in the Okavango Delta, renowned for their luxury and first-rate animal encounters.
- Showcasing the features, exclusive game drives, and supervised activities offered at these resorts.

- Wilderness lodges and tent camps
- Looking for mid-range lodging choices that combine comfort and exposure to the natural beauty of the Delta.
- Talking about guided walking safaris and the "under-canvas" experience.

- Secluded and Private Camps

- Outlining small, isolated campers for visitors looking for privacy and attentive treatment.

- Talking about fly-in safari deals to go to these upscale locations.

What to anticipate

- Giving details on the standard amenities found in lodges and camps, such as private restrooms, eating choices, and terraces from which to observe animals.

- Providing an impression of the surroundings and mood at various sorts of hotels.

4.2 Camping options

- Campsites with self-caterers

- Details about self-catering campgrounds for vacationers looking for a more autonomous and cost-effective experience.

- Talking about kitchen setups, accommodations, and reservation processes.

- Safari camps that are well-equipped
- A description of full-service safari camps created for tourists seeking a camping adventure with more comfort.
- Providing specifics about the tools and services offered.

- Backcountry Camping
- Exploring the pleasure of stargazing while camping in the wilderness.
- Talking about the rules and procedures for safe wild camping.

- Safari camping
- Defining movable camping safaris, in which visitors move from one campground to another.

- Emphasizing the versatility and adventure of this choice.

4.3 Cheap Places to Stay

- Reasonably priced inns and lodges
- Advice for visitors on a tight budget seeking inexpensive lodging choices.
- Mentioning guesthouses as options in neighboring towns.

- Backpacker accommodations and hostels
- Talking about guesthouses and backpacker hostels that serve budget tourists.
- Emphasizing shared spaces, social settings, and community locations.

- Selecting the Appropriate Budget Option
- Giving advice on how to choose a low-cost hotel based on its location, facilities, and closeness to attractions.

-    Stressing   that   inexpensive accommodations may nevertheless provide genuine Delta experiences.

- Advance reservations
- Telling visitors to reserve lodging in advance to take advantage of the greatest offers and availability, particularly those on a tight budget.
- Promoting websites and online booking services for low-cost lodging.

Travelers may get a thorough overview of all the lodging choices in the Okavango Delta in this section, including anything from luxurious resorts to inexpensive campsites and hostels.

Chapter 5

Investigating the Delta

5.1 Safari Adventures

– Vintage Game Drives

- An introduction to traditional game drives in open 4x4 vehicles, which provide chances to see the famous species of the Delta.

- Highlighting the indigenous guides' proficiency in observing and interpreting animal behavior.

- Safaris at night

- Emphasizing the special experience of night safaris, when visitors may see predators and nocturnal animals at work.

- Talking about the use of highlighting methods.

- Safaris on boats
- Investigating safaris from boats around the waterways of the Delta, which provide a distinct viewpoint on the animals and landscape.
- Talking about when to watch water-based games.

Safaris for photographers
- Talking about specialist photography safaris for lovers who wish to shoot the animals and natural beauty of the Delta.
- Bringing up the knowledgeable photographers who guide these excursions.

5.2 Mokoro Excursions

The Mokoro Adventure
- An explanation of the mokoro, a kind of traditional dugout canoe, and its role in Delta exploration.

- Describe the eco-friendly and tranquil atmosphere of mokoro trips.

- Guides and Polers
- Understanding the function of local polers and guides who steer mokoros and impart environmental knowledge.
- Talking about their relationship to the Delta and traditional wisdom.

- Plant and Animal Life at the Water Level
- Showcasing the distinctive viewpoint provided by looking at animals and aquatic plants from the water's surface.
- Talking about the peace and proximity to nature experienced on mokoro expeditions.

5.3 Walking Safaris

- A Lead Walk Throughout the Delta

- An introduction to walking safaris, an opportunity to wander across the sceneries of the Delta.
- Talking about the use of armed and qualified guides as well as safety precautions.

- Foot Tracking Wildlife
- Describes the thrill of following creatures on foot, such as rhinos and elephants.
- Talking on the importance of guiding in providing a secure and instructive environment.

- Walking Birdwatching
- Outlining the benefits of birding on walking safaris, where visitors may get up close and personal with various avian species.
- Mentioning the Delta's varied bird population.

5.4 Opportunities for Birdwatching

- The Avian Paradise of the Delta
- Presenting the Okavango Delta as a top spot for birdwatchers.
- Talking about the range of migratory and resident bird species that may be found in the area.

10 Top Places for Birdwatching
- A list of the Delta's particular places and habitats that provide the best chances for birding.
- Disseminating information about endangered and uncommon species to watch out for.

- Birding Tours Led
- Mentioning the availability of expert ornithologists who lead specialist birding expeditions.

- Talking about how to utilize spotting scopes, binoculars, and field guides.

- Birdlife and conservation
- Emphasizing the value of Delta bird conservation efforts and ways that visitors may help.
- Talking about collaborations with international bird conservation groups.

This section offers a thorough description of the different ways visitors may experience the Okavango Delta, accommodating their varied interests and preferences. These options range from customary game drives and mokoro excursions to walking safaris and birding activities.

Chapter 6

Wildlife Sightings

6.1 Species of Iconic Animals

– Glorious African Elephants

- Declaring African elephants as one of the most recognizable and cherished creatures in the Delta.

- Talking about their family systems, behavior, and importance to the ecology.

- Lions, leopards, and cheetahs are the Big Cats.

- Emphasizing the existence of large cats in the Delta and how they hunt.

- Disseminating information to increase the likelihood of seeing these elusive predators.

- Towering giraffes and graceful giraffes
- Describe the opportunity to see giraffes browsing on trees and their magnificence.
- Giving information on the Delta's reticulated and Masai giraffes.

- Red Lechwe and the elusive Lechwe
- A unique Delta species that has adapted to its wet environment is the lechwe antelope.
- Talking about the greatest places to see the yearly lechwe migration.

- Crocodiles and Hippos, Two Aquatic Wonders
- Talking about the crocodiles and hippos that live in the Delta's rivers.
- Emphasizing their actions and stressing the need for polite watching.

6.2 Conservation Initiatives

- Delta Conservation's Function
- Examining the Okavango Delta's conservation efforts and their relevance.
- Showcasing initiatives and groups committed to protecting the ecology.

Anti-Poaching Initiatives
- Talking about the continuous fight to safeguard endangered species and eliminate poaching.
- Emphasizing the value of community engagement and anti-poaching units.

- Localized Conservation
- Outlining the advantages of sustainable tourism and community-driven conservation initiatives.
- Talking about the benefits of tourism to conservation and local economies.

- Wildlife Rescue and Rehabilitation
- Giving details on Delta's animal rescue and rehabilitation facilities.
- Exchanging success tales about the rescue and release of animals.

6.3 Responsible wildlife viewing

- Reputable Wildlife Viewing Techniques
- Outlining moral and responsible rules for watching animals in the wild.
- Stressing the value of keeping a safe, respectful distance.

- Preventing Disturbing Animals
- Informing visitors about the consequences of causing habitat and animal damage.
- Exchanging knowledge on binocular usage and silent observation.

- Picking reputable tour companies

- Giving advice on how to choose tour companies and guides that value the welfare of animals.

- Encouraging tourists to support environmentally and morally responsible tour operators.

- Wildlife Crime Reporting

- Encouraging visitors to report any suspected wildlife trafficking or poaching activity.

- Providing contact details for the appropriate organizations and authorities.

This section seeks to inform visitors about the Okavango Delta's emblematic animal species, the conservation initiatives in place to save these species, and the significance of responsible wildlife-watching habits to guarantee the survival of this distinctive environment.

Chapter 7

Local Communities and Culture

7.1 Getting Along with the Community

- Okavango Delta Communities That Welcome Visitors
- An overview of the welcoming local communities in the Delta.
- Talking about the readiness to interact and be hospitable to guests.

- Interacting with the Community
- Giving advice on how to interact with locals in an efficient manner, including how to utilize standard greetings and expressions.
- Emphasizing the value of displaying respect and cultural awareness.

- Village Visits and Homestays

- Talking about the chance for visitors to get a taste of local life via homestays and escorted village tours.

- Spreading the advantages of these cultural encounters.

7.2 Cultural Experiences

- Dance and Music from the Past

- Making traditional music and dance performances a focal point of the Delta's culture.

- Making suggestions for the ideal locations to observe and take part in these lively displays.

- Artisan workshops and craft markets

- Showcasing the creative prowess of regional artisans.

- Providing information to tourists about craft fairs and studios where they may buy or make their own souvenirs.

- Oral traditions and storytelling
- Examining the rich storytelling tradition practiced by the neighborhood residents.
- Talking about the custom of transferring information and tales through the generations.

- Cultural Events and Festivals
- Outlining any festivals and activities related to local culture that guests are welcome to attend.
- Giving details on times, places, and importance.

7.3 Supporting Local Communities

- Benefits to the community and responsible tourism
- Stressing the advantages of responsible tourism for regional economies.
- Talking about strategies for community development and income sharing.

- Moral Souvenir Purchasing
- Informing tourists on moral souvenir purchasing, emphasizing the value of helping real regional craftspeople.
- Giving advice on how to choose memorable and eco-friendly souvenirs.

- Volunteering and Community Projects
- Showcasing volunteer and community service activities that let visitors give back.
- Talking about the obligations placed on volunteers.

- Traveling Respectfully

- Offering pointers on how to respect regional traditions and customs when visiting.

- Talking about acceptable clothes, conduct, and cultural awareness.

By fostering connections with local people, displaying cultural events, and advocating support for community development and conservation initiatives, this section hopes to improve visitors' cultural experiences in the Okavango Delta.

Chapter 8

Eating and cooking

8.1 Traditional Okavango Cuisine

- Discovering Regional Flavors

- An introduction to the distinctive tastes of the local food in the Okavango Delta.

- Talking about the impact of local foods and preparation techniques.

Must-Try Recipes

- Showcasing regional specialties like seswaa (pounded beef), morogo (wild spinach), and mopane worms that tourists should try.

- Discussing the meals' cultural importance.

Making Local Delights

- Giving insights into the conventional techniques for preparing meals and cooking.
- Talking about how local communities prepare meals together.

8.2 Options for Dining in the Delta

- Dining in lodges and camps
- Describe the dining atmosphere at Delta lodges and campers.
- Talking about the diversity of menus, which often include both foreign and regional cuisine.

- Riverside Restaurant
- Emphasizing the allure of eating by the canals in the Delta or under a starry sky.
- Talking about the setting and atmosphere of these meal events.

- Sundowners and Bush Dinners
- Investigating the thrill of bush meals and wilderness sundowner beverages.
- Talking about the surroundings, campfire tales, and animal sightings that occurred during these occasions.

- Local markets and restaurants
- Mentioning neighborhood restaurants and food markets where visitors may sample regional cuisine.
- Giving hints to foodies on where to uncover secret treasures.

8.3 Dietary Considerations

- Options for vegetarians and vegans
- Addressing the issue of dietary limitations passengers' access to vegetarian and vegan food.

- Talking about using foods that are acquired locally.

- Special diets and food allergies
- Offering advice to tourists with unique dietary needs or food allergies.
- Promoting in advance contact with hosts and cooks.

- Food and Hygiene Safety
- Informing tourists on the need for good cleanliness and food safety.
- Exchanging advice on how to keep healthy while engaging in gastronomic explorations.

- Trying out new tastes
- Encouraging tourists to take advantage of the chance to sample new and distinctive cuisines.

- Giving suggestions on how to handle strange foods with an open mind.

In addition to addressing nutritional issues to guarantee a pleasurable and secure eating experience, this part intends to expose tourists to the tastes and culinary experiences of the Okavango Delta, from traditional delicacies to contemporary dining alternatives.

Chapter 9

Health and Safety

9.1 Maintaining Your Safety in the Delta

- Wildlife Protection
- Outlining precautions to take to remain secure among wildlife, such as keeping a safe distance from animals.
- Outlining what to do if you come into animals while on a safari.

- Water Security
- Giving safety tips to visitors before they engage in water-based activities like mokoro trips.
- Talking about the value of wearing a life jacket and paying attention to directions.

-Sun Protection

- Stressing the need for sun protection in the warm, bright atmosphere of the Delta.

- Promoting the use of wide-brimmed hats, sunglasses, and sunscreen.

- Water Intake and Loss

- Talking about the difficulties of keeping hydrated in a warm, dry atmosphere.

- Giving advice on how to identify dehydration symptoms and carry a sufficient amount of water.

- Knowledge of Insects and Disease

- Informing tourists about insect-borne illnesses and precautions.

- Talking about the need to wear protective gear and bug repellant.

9.2 Health precautions

- Health Checks and Vaccinations
- A list of the health examinations and immunizations that are advised before visiting the Delta.
- Suggesting that tourists speak with their doctor well in advance.

- Risk and Treatment for Malaria
- Talking about the Delta's malaria danger and the significance of malaria prevention.
- Disseminating information about various anti-malarial drugs.

- Travel First Aid Kit
- Outlining the necessary goods for a trip medical kit, such as first aid kits and prescription drugs.
- Emphasizing the importance of having any essential personal medicines with you.

-Insurance for Travel

- Emphasizing the value of comprehensive travel insurance that provides coverage for evacuations, trip cancellations, and medical emergencies.

- Making suggestions for localized travel insurance companies.

9.3 Emergency Contacts

Emergency Services.

- Offering the Delta's emergency services, such as the police, hospitals, and fire departments, contact information.

- Talking about the capacities and reaction times.

- Plans for evacuation

- Informing visitors of evacuation procedures in the event of a major medical emergency.

- Encouraging visitors to register their vacation plans with local organizations or inns.

- Information about Consulates and Embassies
- Listing the phone numbers for each traveler's embassy or consulate in Botswana.
- Talking about the services they can provide in an emergency.

- Nearby Contacts
- Exchanging local connections, such as those of hotels, travel companies, and guides.
- Encouraging visitors to make arrangements for contact with their hosts.

By presenting important advice on keeping safe, taking health measures, and providing emergency contact information for peace of mind while traveling, this section seeks to protect the safety and well-being of tourists in the Okavango Delta.

Chapter 10

Essentials and Packing

10.1 What to Bring

- Clothing Requirements

- Including a thorough list of wardrobe essentials for each season, such as layers for chilly weather and light, breathable clothes for hot weather.

- Stressing the need to bring neutral-colored clothing for safaris.

- Shoewear

- Suggesting footwear that is both cozy and reliable for boat trips and walking safaris.

- Talking about the need for hiking boots and closed-toe shoes.

- Private Items

- Making suggestions for consumables including toiletries, medicines, and personal care goods.

- Proposing eco-friendly and biodegradable product use in the Delta.

- Packing and Luggage Advice

- Giving suggestions for the right kind of baggage to bring, such as transport-friendly soft-sided bags.

- Exchanging packing advice, such as the use of dry bags and packing cubes.

10.2 Important Equipment

Safari Equipment

- Providing information about key safari equipment, such as binoculars, cameras, and field guides.

- Providing details on the kinds of equipment that improve wildlife-watching opportunities.

- Gear for camping
- Giving tourists who want to camp in the Delta a list of the required camping supplies.
- Talking about the equipment that may be rented in Maun.

- First Aid Kit
- A description of the components of a thorough travel medical kit and the significance of bringing one.
- Offering advice on products such as bandages, antiseptics, and insect repellants.

- Electrical and Electronic
- Informing visitors to pack chargers, power adapters, and other power sources.

- Talking about the lodges' and the Delta's access to electricity.

10.3 Travel Advice

- Pack Light
- Reminding tourists to pack lightly and to stay away from carrying too much luggage.
- Offering guidance on how to dress for versatility.

- Dressing Seasonally
- Suggesting weather-appropriate attire, such as lightweight and breathable materials for hot weather.
- Recommending layering for chilly nights.

Practices for Sustainable Travel
- Talking about environmentally beneficial travel habits, such as minimizing plastic

waste and encouraging eco-friendly lodging.

- Encouraging tourists to have a minimal influence on the environment.

- Passport Documents
- Reminding passengers to bring copies of their key documents and the necessary travel documentation, such as their passports and visas.
- Stressing the significance of preventing theft or damage to these papers.

- Currency and Banking in the Area
- Giving advice on how to manage your money in the Delta, including details on the local currency and banking options.
- Talking about the locations where ATMs may be found.

This section tries to provide tourists with a thorough breakdown of what to bring, necessary equipment to improve their adventures, and useful travel advice to make their trip to the Okavango Delta comfortable and pleasant.

Chapter 11

Environmental Protection

11.1 Safeguarding the Okavango Delta

- The Delta's Exposure

- Showcasing the Okavango Delta's distinctive and vulnerable ecology.

- Talking about the environmental dangers the Delta faces, such as habitat loss and climate change.

- Environmental Protection Groups

- Outlining significant conservation groups and projects protecting the Delta.

- Exchanging information about their goals, initiatives, and contributions to conservation efforts.

- Environmental regulations

- Providing a summary of local laws and policies intended to protect the natural beauty of the Delta.

- Talking about the rules for responsible travel.

- Traveler Obligations

- Informing visitors about their responsibility for preserving the Delta, such as by respecting nature and animals.

- Promoting moral conduct and obedience to rules.

11.2 Sustainable Travel Practices

- Environmentally friendly lodging

- Suggesting sustainable resorts and campgrounds in the Delta that are eco-friendly.

- Talking about techniques like solar power, water saving, and waste minimization.

- Cutting Down Plastic Waste
- Giving tips to tourists on how to reduce their use of plastics while traveling.
- Talking about the value of reusable shopping bags and water bottles.

- Promoting Neighborhood Communities
- Talking about the advantages of promoting regional communities via responsible tourism.
- Showcasing community-based tourism projects that help locals and visitors alike.

- Offsetting Carbon
- Examining the idea of carbon offsetting and the ways that tourists may help to lessen their carbon impact.

- Mentioning initiatives that emphasize sustainable energy and forestry.

11.3 Preservation of Wildlife

- Anti-Poaching Initiatives and Poaching
- Talking about the Delta's vulnerability to poaching and the significance of anti-poaching efforts.
- Exchanging success tales and poaching prevention techniques.

- Locally Driven Conservation
- Showcasing community-based conservation efforts and their beneficial effects on the preservation of wildlife.
- Talking about how local communities should manage the land.

- Viewing of Ethical Wildlife

- Stressing ethical and acceptable wildlife-watching techniques.

- Outlining rules for keeping a respectful and safe distance from animals.

- Assistance with conservation initiatives

- Encouraging visitors to donate money or give their time to help protect animals.

- Talking about how ecotourism contributes to the financing of conservation activities.

The purpose of this part is to inform visitors about the significance of environmental preservation in the Okavango Delta and to provide advice on how to travel sustainably with the least possible negative effect on the environment and local populations.

Chapter 12

Organizing Your Travel

12.1 Sample Itineraries

- Three to four-day getaway
- Giving visitors with little time to experience the Delta an example itinerary.
- Showcasing the must-do activities and sights for a brief stay.

- 7–10 Days for the Classic Delta Experience
- Providing a thorough program for a traditional Delta experience, which includes safari excursions and cultural encounters.
- Talking about a healthy balance of activity and downtime.

- 2 weeks or more of extended exploration

- Providing a more extensive itinerary for those who want to explore the Delta in detail.

- Offering possibilities for extra activities and day excursions.

An Adventure That Is Family-Friendly

- Making recommendations for a family-friendly plan that includes kid-friendly activities.

- Talking about resorts and activities for kids.

12.2 Personalized Travel Options

- Customizing Your Trip

- Encouraging visitors to modify their trip plans in accordance with their own interests and preferences.

- Talking about how flexible travel is on the Delta.

- Activity Choice
- Giving advice on choosing pursuits that fit a person's interests, such as wildlife safaris, cultural excursions, or adventure sports.
- Talking about the value of diversity in the itinerary.

- Particular Interests and Subjects
- Emphasizing specialty itineraries, such as those for romantic vacations, birding, or photography.
- Talking about how to design a vacation around a certain set of interests.

- Using a travel agent for planning
- Promoting the usage of neighborhood travel agents with knowledge of Delta Travel.

- Outlining the advantages of expert advice.

12.3 Planning a Budget

- Making a Budget
- Giving advice on how to create a reasonable Okavango Delta vacation budget.
- Talking about the various prices for lodging, entertainment, and meals.

- Money-Saving Advice
- Providing advice on how to save costs for travelers, such as suggesting that they go off-peak or stay in cheap hotels.
- Talking about the benefits of all-inclusive vacation packages.

- Secret Charges

- Informing visitors about possible unforeseen expenses such as park fees, extra activities, and gratuities.

- Financial planning guidance to pay for these costs.

- Cash Reserves

- Advise vacationers to set aside emergency monies for unforeseen circumstances.

- Talking about how to utilize cash and credit cards in the Delta.

Whether a visitor has a limited amount of time or prefers a more in-depth tour, this section is intended to help them create their optimal itinerary for the Okavango Delta. To assist guests in making the most of their trip, it offers example itineraries, modification advice, and financial preparation.

Chapter 13

Conclusion

13.1 Remembering the Okavango Delta

- Treasure Memorable Experiences
- Thinking back on the distinctive experiences that visitors to the Okavango Delta may look forward to.
- Inspiring vacationers to document and cherish their experiences.

- Spending time in nature
- Showcasing the Delta's deep connection to animals and the natural world.
- Inspiring vacationers to cherish these ties even after they've gone back home.

- Encounters with Local Cultures

- Thinking back on the cross-cultural exchanges and links with the neighborhood communities.

- Discussing how cultural experiences have a lasting influence.

13.2 Final Advice and Suggestions

- Ongoing Support for Conservation

- Encouraging tourists to continue supporting Delta environmental protection activities.

- Talking about strategies to continue participating and contributing even after the adventure is over.

- Telling Your Tales

- Inspiring and educating others by encouraging travelers to share their experiences and stories.

- Endorsing social media, travel blogs, and travel discussion forums as sharing venues.

- Follow-Up Visits
- Encouraging visitors to think about returning to the Okavango Delta for various seasons and novel encounters.
- Talking about the benefit of seeing familiar places with new eyes.

- Keeping Current
- Suggesting that visitors keep up with any changes to the laws, lodgings, or activities in the Delta.
- Giving instructions on how to get the most recent updates.

13.3 Goodbye and safe travels

- A Heartfelt Farewell

- Bidding a fond goodbye to those who have used the guide's aid to tour the Okavango Delta.
- Wishing that the beauty of the Delta will live on in their hearts.

Best Regards and Safe Travels
- Sending well wishes to all travelers, whether they are going farther on their trip or coming home.
- Reminding them to always take their memories with them.

- Contact Details
- Giving the author or organization of the travel guide's contact information in case you have any queries or need more help.
- Requesting comments and ideas for the next enhancements.

This part concludes the trip guide by providing readers with enduring memories, helpful suggestions, and well-wishes for their next explorations of the Okavango Delta.

Printed in Great Britain
by Amazon

33594378R00046